AHAYAH YASHARAHLA JUDAH, BENJAMIN AND LEVI

TARA LA SEAN

Ahayah Yasharahla

Judah, Benjamin and Levi

An Advanced *My Time With The Most High* Workbook

By

Tara La Sean

The Lord's Prayer

Our Father (Ahayah) which art in Heaven, Hallowed be thy name. Thy kingdom come, Thy will be done in earth, as it is in Heaven. Give us this day our daily bread. And forgive us our debts as we forgive our debtors. And lead us not into temptation, but deliver us from evil: For thine is the kingdom, and the power, and the glory, forever.

Ahayah Bahasham Yashaya Wa Rawach

(In the name of the Father, the Son and the Holy Spirit)

Amen

Shalom Brothers and Sisters!

It gives me great pleasure to present this latest segment of the *My Time With The Most High* workbook series! Much like the first four books of this series which gives Bible students a variety of puzzles, activities and writing prompts to help retain information about the Creation of the Universe, our history, heritage and the Law, this series is a guide to better understanding the various actions and attributes of the 12 brothers who are the predecessors of all Israelites.

Although this series features many of same types of activities as the original and can be used by learners of all ages, Ahayah Yasharalah is geared toward more advanced students. To complete the activities in this section you will need the KJV Bible, The Apocrypha, the Testament of the Twelve Patriarchs and the Book of Jasher (as translated by R.H. Charles).* This section assumes that you have read these records and are at least familiar with the content. As an extra challenge, some activities may require you to search the internet to help answer questions.

 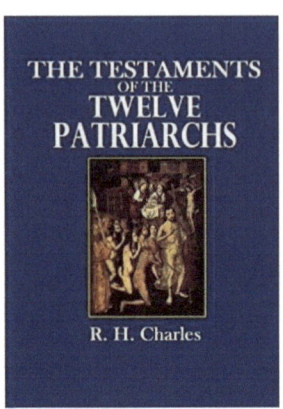 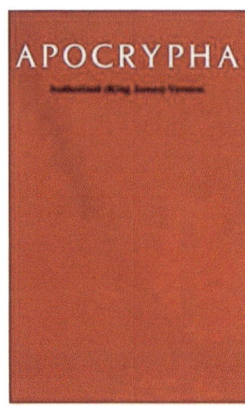 

I hope you will continue to study the Word and learn more about our Magnificent Power, Ahayah, as well as our rich history and colorful foreparents!

Barak Atha!

Sis Tara~

*If you do not have these records by R.H. Charles, you can download them for free as a PDF to your personal device.

http://www.earlychristianwritings.com/text/patriarchs-charles.html

http://www.parsontom.com/books/Book%20of%20Jasher.pdf

Part One:

Judah; The King

Judah: Line of Kings

Complete the crossword below using the KJV, Testament of Patriarchs and Book of Jasher

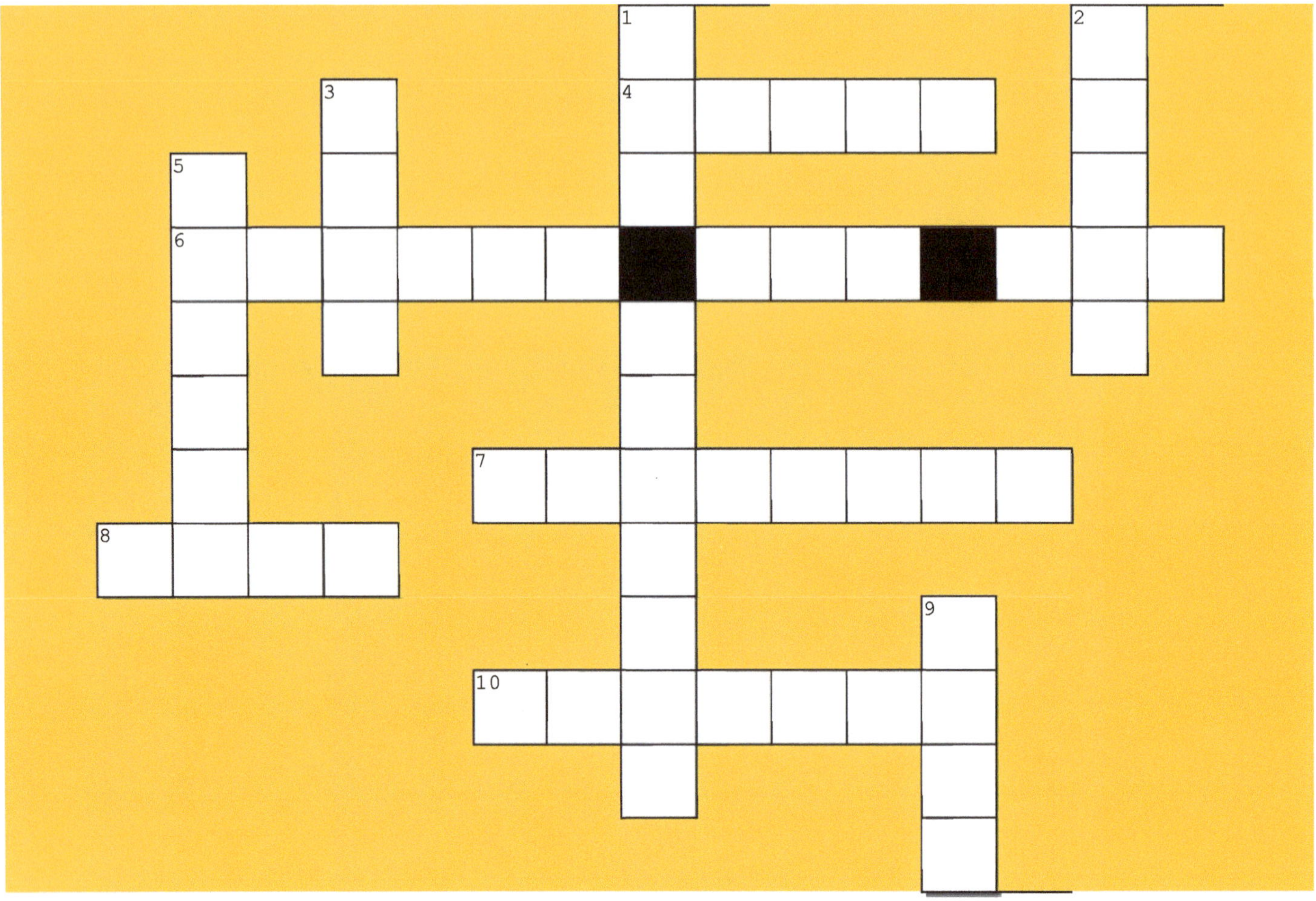

Created with TheTeachersCorner.net Crossword Puzzle Generator

Across

4. Judah is a lion's ___________

6. Which two brothers fought with Judah against the sons of Esau when he climbed a ladder and slew four mighty men? 3 words)

7. Judah is compared to what is Isaiah 5?

8. Who is Judah's mother?

10. What shall never depart from Judah?

Down

1. When Judah and his brothers captured Hazor, how many men did he slay? (2 words)

2. Where was Judah's wife from?

3. What number son is Judah?

5. What does the name Judah mean?

9. What animal did Judah take by the paw and hurl off a cliff?

Challenge! For question 5 Down, write the answer in Hebrew and give the Strong's Concordance reference!

____

____

____

____

The Passions of Judah...

Why did Ahayah strike Onan down?
_____
_____
_____
_____
_____

What type of woman was Bathshua? Give details about her character and her bloodline.
_____
_____
_____
_____
_____

On at least **two** occasions Judah became drunk and made a bad decision concerning women. Describe them.
_____
_____
_____
_____
_____

Deeper Dive: Research the law concerning a childless widow and how that law related to Onan, Judah and the parentage of Joseph in the New Testament.

Watch Your Daughters!

In the Testament of the Twelve Patriarchs, Judah gathers his sons and gives them a serious warning about what would befall their daughters. Discuss what that prophecy was and how it has come true. Give at least three examples.

From Leading a Flock to Leading a Nation; The Boy Who Would be King

YOUNG DAVID: AHAYAH APPOINTED; PROPHET ANOINTED

1. Who was David's best friend?
   _____

2. What instrument did David play to help the king sleep? Name the king and why he had trouble sleeping.
   _____
   _____
   _____

3. Which prophet anointed David? _____

4. How many older brothers did David have and what were their names?
   _____
   _____
   _____

5. What weapon did David wield to bring down the giant? _____

6. What two animals did David slay with his bare hands?
   _____

David was a very talented singer, songwriter and musician. Choose one of the songs he wrote and discuss the meaning of the lyrics. Challenge: Include additional information on location and the history of Israel during the period David wrote the piece.

_____
_____
_____
_____
_____
_____
_____
_____
_____
_____
_____
_____
_____
_____

Seek out Judah

Find the hidden words in this puzzle.

ROYALTY
KINGSHIP
CROUCHING
FOURTH
LEADERSHIP
STRENGTH

SCEPTRE
LION
SOUTHERN
FIERCE
ELECT

LAWGIVER
YASHAYA
PRAISE
POWERFUL
DOMINION

Words of Judah

Use Gen. 49 and the Testament of the 12 Patriarchs to fill in the sentences.

Created on TheTeachersCorner.net Fill-in-the-Blank Maker

> money, deceit   Amorites
>
> ordinances   craftiness
>
> fornication   Mesopotamia
>
> brethren   Canaanites

1. I, therefore, and Dan feigned ourselves to be _____, and as allies went into their city.

2. Of Er: And he had not known her according to the evil _____ of his mother.

3. And now, I command you, my children, not to love _____ nor to gaze upon the beauty of women;

4. Judah, thou art he whom thy _____ shall praise:

5. . And the works of truth and the works of _____ are written upon the hearts of men, and each one of them the Lord knoweth

6. And I knew the race of the _____ was wicked, but the impulse of youth blinded my mind.

7. And after these things my son Er took to wife Tamar, from _____, a daughter of Aram.

8. …,and keep my sayings to perform all the _____ of the Lord. And to obey the commands of God.

9. For the spirit of _____ hath wine as a minister.

12

When your *Mother* is an O. G. Judite...
Your heart cannot pump Kool-Aid!

STRENGTH, COURAGE AND FAITH: MAMA MACABEE WAS PURE JUDAH!

We have read countless stories about the courage, wisdom and unwavering trust in Ahayah that many of our male Judahite ancestors possessed. Read 2 Macabee Chapter 7 to learn about this remarkable woman and her extraordinary sons. Define each of the following terms and discuss how the mother of the Seven Martyrs exemplified each characteristic. For an additional challenge, find other Biblical Judahites who share the same attribute.

1. Courage:

2. Faith:

3. Wisdom:

4. Strength:

5. Encouragement:

Judah: Then and Now...

Search the scriptures for one descendant from the tribe of Judah and find one historical or current figure. Using what you know about the strengths and weaknesses of this tribe, discuss how your selected persons are examples of those characteristics.

_____
_____
_____
_____
_____
_____
_____
_____
_____
_____
_____
_____
_____
_____
_____
_____
_____
_____
_____
_____
_____
_____
_____
_____
_____
_____
_____
_____

Part Two:

Levi; The Priest

And the 'Best Dressed' Award goes to...

Read Chapter 8 of the Testament of Levi. Describe the garments put on him by the seven men in white and compare it to the garment Aaron was given in Exodus.

THE RISE, REIGN AND RUIN OF LEVI

1. Give **two** details from each of the three visions concerning Levi becoming priest.

   Vision 1-
   _____
   _____

   Vision 2-
   _____
   _____

   Vision 3-
   _____
   _____

2. Give at least one example of the duties of the priesthood as described from each of the following books: Exodus, Leviticus and Numbers.

   Exodus-
   _____
   _____
   _____

   Leviticus-
   _____
   _____
   _____

   Numbers-
   _____
   _____
   _____

3. Review Genesis 49 and the 12 Patriarchs Testament of Levi. Give at least 3 examples from scripture that prove who the modern-day Levites are.

   _____
   _____
   _____
   _____
   _____
   _____

Priesthood Crossword

Read Genesis 49, Book of Jasher chapter 37 and the Testament of Levi to answer the following questions.

Across
3. Besides Levi, who else saw a vision of him become the priest of Israel?
6. In his vision, TMH told Levi He was being given what blessing?
8. How old was Levi when he went into the land of Canaan?
9. Who would Levi become a scorn to in the last days?

Down
1. Which brother did he fight against the men of Shechem with?
2. What number son was Levi?
4. Levi warned his sons that out of _____ would they teach the commandments of the Lord.
5. In the latter days, what type of instruments would be found in the habitations of Levi?
7. Who was his mother
10. Who was the king of Gaash that Levi slew?

Bonus question: How old was Levi's daughter Jochebed when she got married?

Fill In for Levi!

Read Gen. Ch. 49, Deut. Ch 33 and Mal. Ch 2 to fill in the blanks. Use the words in the list below to complete the sentence.

1. Simeon and Levi are brother; _____ of _____ are in their dwelling.
2. The law of _____ was in his mouth.
3. For the lips of a priest should keep _____ and people should _____ the law from his mouth.
4. Behold I will _____ your decedents and spread _____ on their faces.
5. My covenant was with him, one of _____ and _____ and I have them to him that he might fear Me…
6. Let your _____ and your _____ be with the Holy One…
7. _____ be their anger, for it is fierce; and their _____ for it is cruel.

WORD BANK

Warning: Not all words below are correct answers!

BLESSED CURSED RAISE ASHES INSTRUMENTS PRAISE REBUKE LIGHT TRUTH REFUSE FAITH URIM WRATH KNOWLEDGE SANCTIFY THUMMIN CRUELTY DEATH LIFE LOVE PEACE SEEK

Aaron: Big Brother, Master Orator, High Priest of a Nation

ALL ABOUT AARON

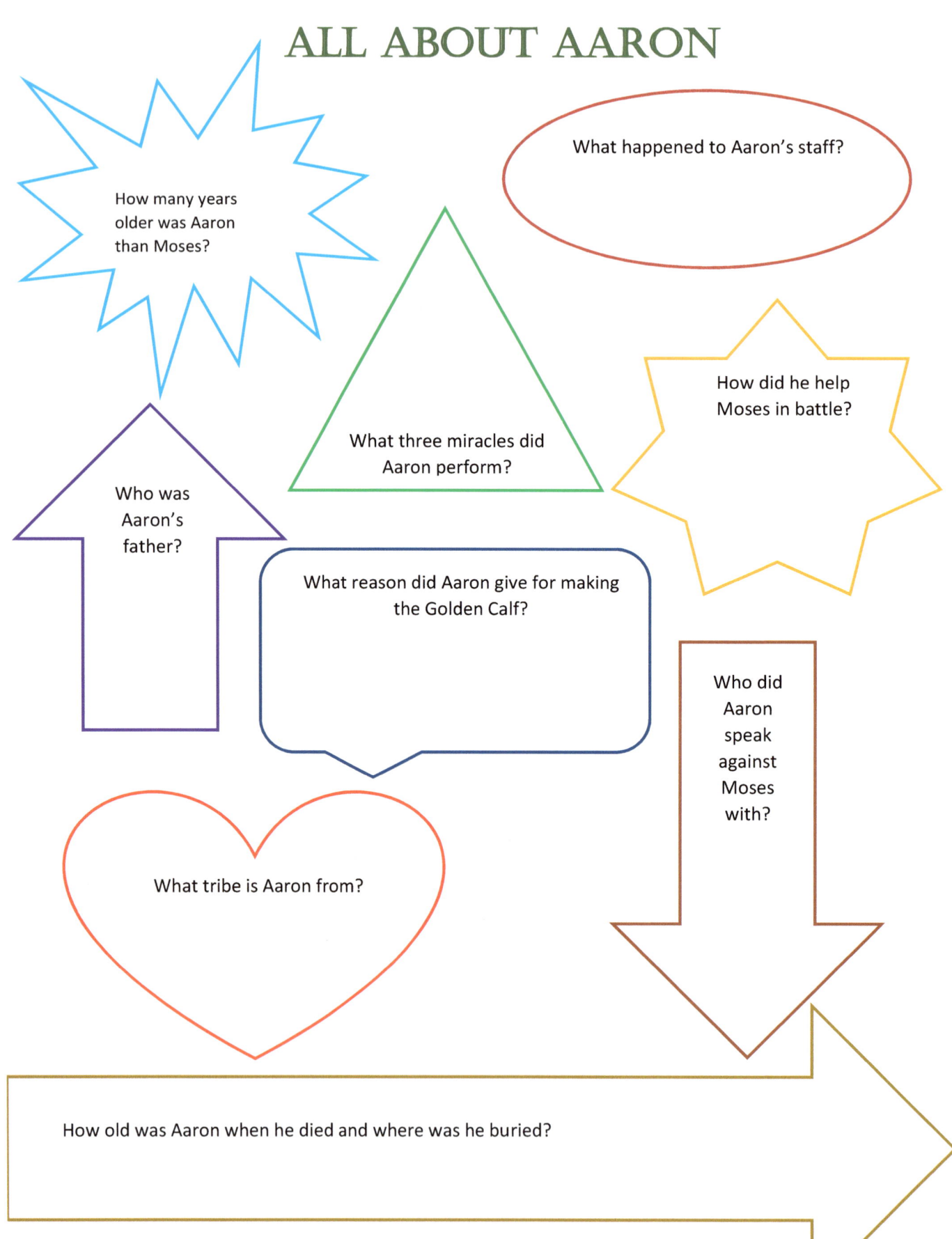

In Search of Levi
Search for hidden words associated with Levi in this puzzle.

CURSED	BLESSED	MESSENGER
PRIESTHOOD	THUMMIN	URIM
SACRIFICE	ALTER	ORDAINED
INIQUITY	KNOWLEDGE	PEACE
LIFE	VISIONS	INHERITANCE
LAW	JUDGEMENT	MITRE
SACRED	WRATH	

Instruments of Cruelty

The Tribe of Levi was very special to TMH and He gave them gifts in the spiritual realm to act as priests for the nation. After the fall of the Northern and Southern kingdoms, Levi was taken into captivity by the Spaniards to present-day Haiti (and later to New Orleans, Louisiana.) Watch the following 39-minute YouTube clip titled **Haitian Voodoo Witchcraft (Evil Spirits)** (https://www.youtube.com/watch?v=g-IwdOgSgF8&t=1338s) and answer the questions below (assume this person's account is accurate). Be sure to include at least ***three*** precepts) from any Hebrew record to support your position.

1. Curtis Kelly explained that night terrors are demonic attacks. Do you agree?

2. He points out that when curses go out, they also come back on the person cursing. Do you believe this is true? And if so, what impact do you think this has on the overall condition of Haitians today?

3. Mr. Curtis makes a point of showing how the local Voodoo priestess was known as a "Christian evangelist" and all her customers were part of the Christian church. Why do you think mainstream Christians readily accepts help from witches and members of the occult?

4. Another interesting point he made was that familiar spirits inhabited inanimate objects. Do you think this is possible? If so, what would this tell us about the use of statuary in all religions from Catholicism and Christianity to Islam and Buddhism?

Miracles, Mamas and The Most High...

Elizabeth: Righteous Daughter of Levi

The story of Elizabeth, mother of John the Baptist, is a beautiful and inspiring tale of how joy is one of the rewards of patience and perseverance when following The Most High. Just as the men from the Tribe of Levi are known for their deep spiritual connection with TMH, their understanding of the Law and the favor they have of The Most High, so too do many of the women from this tribe enjoy these traits. Read the story of Elizabeth from the account of Luke and define the characteristics below. Discuss how Elizabeth was an example of each trait. As an extra challenge, the attributes are given in Hebrew! Include the Strong's definition and number in your answers.

1. Yiqhah:

2. Chen:

3. Amanah:

4. Berakah:

5. Reuth:

BENJAMIN: THE WARRIOR

MY BROTHER; MY HERO

Benjamin thought very highly of his big brother Joseph. After reading the Testament of Benjamin and the full story of Joseph's captivity and subsequent rise in Egypt (Gen. 37-45), do you think Benjamin was right to revere him? Give at least three examples of why Benjamin looked up to Joseph. Describe their relationship and the impact it had on what Benjamin told his sons in his own testament.

YOUNGEST SON OF A YOUNGEST SON

Use the KJV Bible and the Testament of Benjamin to answer the questions below.

1. Who was Benjamin referring to in chapter 11 of the Testament of Benjamin? Give two examples of how you know.

   _____
   _____
   _____

2. Give two examples of how you know who the modern day Benjaminites are.

   _____
   _____
   _____
   _____

Give two examples of how we know Benjamin was part of the Southern Kingdom.

_____
_____
_____
_____
_____

Baby Brother Benjamin

Use all of your resources to help you answer the questions and solve the puzzle!

Across
4. Jacob compared Benjamin to what animal?
6. How much coin did Joseph give Benjamin? (2words)
7. Who was Benjamin's mother?
9. The name Benjamin means 'son of' what in Hebrew? (2-words)
10. Which brother offered his own life for the life of Benjamin in Egypt?

Down
1. What possession of Joseph's was Benjamin accused of stealing? (2 words)
2. How long was his mother barren after having Joseph? (2 words)
3. Who suckled Benjamin after his mother died?
5. How many sons did Benjamin have?
8. Benjamin's bones were taken to Hebron during which war?

Wisdom of a Warrior

Use the words below to complete the scriptures.

Created on TheTeachersCorner.net Fill-in-the-Blank Maker

Word Bank
mind light peace ravin
glorified, dark punished
sinners. heaven…
mercy envy judgment
reverence prophecy
commandments.
confirmation, truth
brethren angel right

1. Because for ever those who are like Cain in _____ and hatred of _____ shall be _____ with the same judgement.

2. …, for the _____ of _____ guideth his soul.

3. If any one is _____ he envieth him not;

4. Benjamin shall _____ like the wolf:

5. …for he that hath his mind _____ seeth all things rightly.

6. _____ In thee shall be fulfilled the _____ of _____

7. _____ For the good man hath not a _____ eye; for he showeth _____ to all men, even though they be _____

8. For where there is _____ for good works and _____ in the mind, even darkness fleeth

9. Do ye, therefore, _____ and righteousness each one to his neighbor, and _____ unto _____ and keep the law of the Lord and His _____

10. Let your _____ be unto good.

31

FAITHFUL FRIEND, FORTUNATE FISHERMAN, FEARLESS FIGHTER

Peter: Yashaya's Ride or Die Disciple

Examine the following scriptures and discuss what each one says about Peter and the special relationship Yashaya had with him.

1. John 21:15-17

2. Matt. 16: 13-20

3. John 18: 10-11

4. Mark 1: 16-18

5. John 13: 6-9

"HEY BULLY; I'M GONNA TELL MY *KID BROTHER* ON YOU!"

So far, much has been said about the Benjaminites being warriors. But what more does the Bible say about them? Research the following passages and determine if they are about Benjamin (and his descendants) or not. For the scriptures that do pertain to the battle prowess of this tribe, write out the verse and how it relates. For the rest, write out who the passage refers to.

1. **Acts 9:5**

2. **2 Chronicles 17:17**

3. **Is. 63:3**

4. **Rev. 19:13**

5. **1 Chron. 8:40**

6. **Ps. 144:1**

7. **Judges 20:46**

8. **1 Chron. 12:2**

9. **Neh. 13:21**

10. **Gen. 14:15**

Beware of the DARKSIDE...

We have learned that Benjamin was a mighty warrior, skilled with the bow and the sword. However, in his testament before dying he warned his sons not to fall into the "evils of war and bloodshed." Review chapter 7 of his testament and Judges, chapters 19-21. Why do you think it was necessary for Benjamin to warn his children against the evils of war?

Wisdom of a Warrior Remix!

Use the 20 answers from the previous fill-in activity to solve the word search puzzle!

```
C F Y P P L S Q K J E T B J I N C F C D
S R X E J M N R M V S M A B Y Q Q O K W
T O A U Z U F B W Y S I G U E N V Y B V
N C U Z R Z M E C T N X C A O B Y B X E
E E F R T Z O Z D M N E H I U U B X Q H
M C N R M F H Z E J H E T K I O T U N P
D N G D O O G T V J X A M L D L U M G E
N E B T B P G O U M M U V R Q G V K T F
A R D N I M I W B R I G H T D P O U I Y
M E J E K J Z N I J T M N Z E U E R W N
M V X G Q B G F C S P T P M G N J B M H
O E B P L M N D E L B B R A H I T P S F
C R R O E O L T E J G K O E F S K B X C
Y X N J C M R G F O W L P K E H K R U D
L S S R E N N I S Q I N H L W E S E A H
S Q K R U A I P F G Y G E I V D T L D
U X C U E S C V H I M H C V O J R H H J
J Y C F F R E T A R E F Y T A R L R B G
E U M L S I E X P R Y D O P G E M E Y I
I V I K H O U X Q S D F T U Q G H N T L
```

BENJAMIN: THEN AND NOW...

As students of Bible scripture, Israelite history and Hebrew culture, we know that Jamaica is one of the 'New World' areas heavily populated by the Tribe of Benjamin. Watch the following 12-minute YouTube video about the Maroons titled *The Maroons: Jamaica's Forgotten Nation* (https://www.youtube.com/watch?v=LJfVfH09SK8). The short clip gives several examples of how we know the true Israelite identity of modern-day Jamaicans. Pick at least **_three_** of those examples and precept it with at least **_two_** scriptures from any valid Hebrew record.

Example 1.
___

Precept 1.
___

Precept 2.
___

Example 2.
___

Precept 1.
___

Precept 2.
___

Example 3.
___

Precept 1.
___

Precept 2.
___

Bravery AND Beauty? She must be a Benjamite!

Esther: Israel's Warrior Queen

By now, we all understand that the Benjaminites were a tribe of mighty men who were bonafide warriors. But what about the ladies of the tribe? Were they as fierce as their men? Before you start imagining the Dahomey women warriors of West Africa, let's examine the book of Esther. But first, to help us determine the characteristics of a warrior, read the article: *10 QUALITIES OF A MODERN DAY WARRIOR* by fitness guru Chad Howse (https://chadhowsefitness.com/2013/09/10-qualities-of-a-modern-day-warrior). Chose **_five_** attributes and explain how Esther, in all of her righteous femininity, exemplified that attribute.

Wrap-Up

A final word from the prophets...

It is interesting to note that most of the prophets were from the Southern Kingdom and of the tribes of Levi, Benjamin and Judah. Research the following prophets and tell which tribe they were from and give at least **_two_** of their most notable actions or prophecies.

1. **Isaiah:**
   _____
   _____
   _____

2. **Jeremiah:**
   _____
   _____
   _____

3. **Nehemiah:**
   _____
   _____
   _____

4. **Baruch:**
   _____
   _____
   _____

5. **Ezekiel:**
   _____
   _____
   _____

6. **Daniel:**
   _____
   _____
   _____

Shalawam Family,

I certainly hope you enjoyed the first book in the Ahayah Yasharalah series! When TMH first gave me the idea to begin studying the 12 Patriarchs, I was very excited and couldn't wait to share all I'd learned with you. What is even more special to me is the enthusiastic support I have received from my home church in Dallas and the willingness of so many of my brothers, sisters and even my Bishop to participate in this project. Instead of scouring the internet for pictures to illustrate these workbooks, I am now able to present pictures featuring my beautiful family! I thank each and every one of you for lending your time and talents; from modeling and photography to the creation of garments for our wardrobe. May Ahayah bless you all for your dedication!

I salute you!

Barak Athan & Thawadah!

Sis Tara

Answers

Judah; Line of Kings

Complete the crossword below using the KJV, Testament of Patriarchs and Book of Jasher

						1 t							2 c
		3 f			4 w	h	e	l	p				a
5 p		o				o							a
6 r	e	u	b	e	n		a	n	d		g	a	d
a		r				h							n
i						u							
s					7 v	i	n	e	y	a	r	d	
8 l	e	a	h			d							
						r				9 b			
				10 s	c	e	p	t	r	e			
						d				a			
										r			

Created with TheTeachersCorner.net Crossword Puzzle Generator

Across

4. Judah is a lion's _____ (**whelp**)
6. Which two brothers fought with Judah against the sons of Esau when he climbed a ladder and slew four mighty men? 3 words) (**reuben and gad**)
7. Judah is compared to what is Isaiah 5? (**vineyard**)
8. Who is Judah's mother? (**leah**)
10. What shall never depart from Judah? (**sceptre**)

Down

1. When Judah and his brothers captured Hazor, how many men did he slay? (2 words) (**two hundred**)
2. Where was Judah's wife from? (**caaan**)
3. What number son is Judah? (**four**)
5. What does the name Judah mean? (**praise**)
9. What animal did Judah take by the paw and hurl off a cliff? (**bear**)

Seek out Judah
Find the hidden words in this puzzle.

44

All About Aaron

1. 3 Years older
2. Staff budded, blossomed and bore almonds
3. Water to blood, Frogs, Gnats
4. Amram
5. The people were set on mischief
6. Held up his arms
7. Tribe of Levi
8. His sister Miriam
9. 123 years, Meribah

In Search of Levi
Search for hidden words associated with Levi in this puzzle.

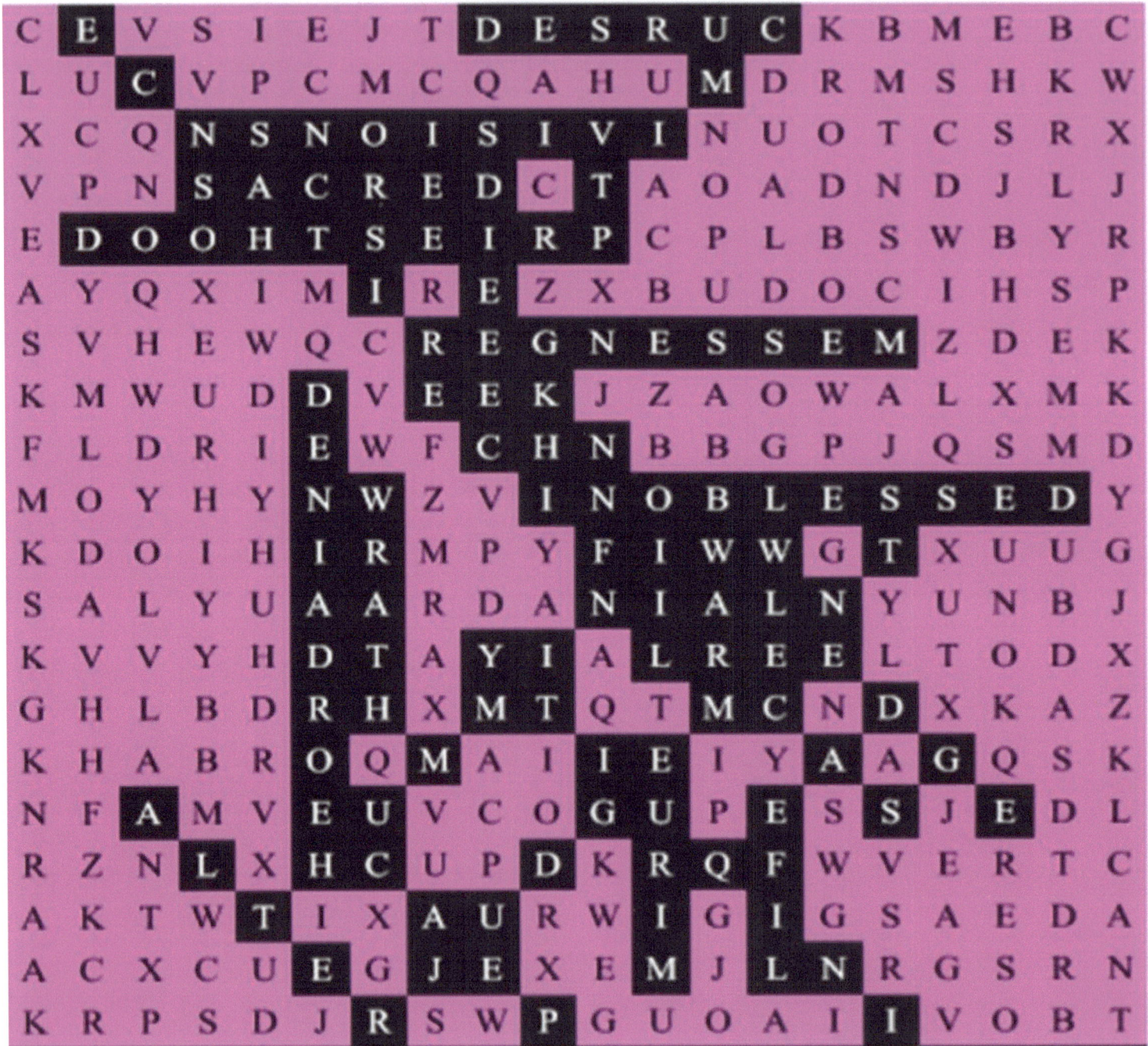

Priesthood Crossword

Read Genesis 49, Book of Jasher chapter 37 and the Testament of Levi to answer the following questions.

								¹s		²t
	³j	a	⁴c	o	b			i		h
			o					m		i
		⁵c		v				e		r
	⁶p	r	i	e	s	t	h	o	o	d
		u		t				n		
		e		o						
⁷l		l		u						
⁸e	i	g	h	t						
a				y						
h				s						
				n		⁹g	e	n	t	i	l	¹⁰e	s
				s								l
				s								o
												n

Created with TheTeachersCorner.net Crossword Puzzle Generator

Fill in for Levi!

Read Gen. Ch. 49, Deut. Ch 33 and Mal. Ch 2 to fill in the blanks. Use the words in the list below to complete the sentence.

> instruments refuse seek cruelty Cursed rebuke peace life Urim truth knowledge, wrath Thummin

1. Simeon and Levi and brothers; __instruments__ of __cruelty__ are in their dwelling.
2. The law of __truth__ was in his mouth...
3. For the lips of a priest should keep __knowledge,__ and people should __seek__ the law from his mouth.
4. _____ Behold, I will __rebuke__ your descendants and spread __refuse__ on your faces....
5. . My covenant was with him, one of __life__ and __peace__ and I gave them to him that he might fear Me...
6. Let your __Thummin__ and your __Urim__ be with Your holy one.....
7. __Cursed__ be their anger, for it is fierce; and their __wrath__ for it is cruel!

Baby Brother Benjamin
Use all of your resources to help you answer the questions and solve the puzzle!

Created with TheTeachersCorner.net Crossword Puzzle Generator

Wisdom of a Warrior Remix!

Use the 20 answers from the previous fill-in activity to solve the word search puzzle!

Wisdom of a Warrior

Use the words below to complete the scriptures.

Created on TheTeachersCorner.net Fill-in-the-Blank Maker

Word Bank
mind light peace ravin
glorified, dark punished
sinners. heaven…
mercy envy judgment
reverence prophecy
commandments.
confirmation, truth
brethren angel right

1. Because for ever those who are like Cain in __envy__ and hatred of __brethren__ shall be __punished__ with the same judgement.
2. …, for the __angel__ of __peace__ guideth his soul.
3. If any one is __glorified,__ he envieth him not;
4. Benjamin shall __ravin__ like the wolf:
5. …for he that hath his mind __right__ seeth all things rightly.
6. _____ In thee shall be fulfilled the __prophecy__ of __heaven…__
7. _____ For the good man hath not a __dark__ eye; for he showeth __mercy__ to all men, even though they be __sinners.__
8. For where there is __reverence__ for good works and __light__ in the mind, even darkness fleeth
9. Do ye, therefore, __truth__ and righteousness each one to his neighbor, and __judgment__ unto __confirmation,__ and keep the law of the Lord and His __commandments.__
10. Let your __mind__ be unto good.